ALSO BY AISHAH RAHMAN

Plays

LADY DAY: A MUSICAL TRAGEDY
THE MOJO AND THE SAYSO
ONLY IN AMERICA
TALE OF MADAME ZORA

One Acts

Mingus Takes (3)
IF ONLY WE KNEW
THE LADY AND THE TRAMP
SPEAKER'S HEAD

Novel

Pigmentocracy Blues

Memoir

Chewed Water

Libretto

ANYBODY SEEN MARIE LAVEAU?

UNFINISHED WOMEN CRY IN NO MAN'S LAND
WHILE A BIRD DIES IN A GILDED CAGE was first
produced by the New York Shakespeare Festival in
June 1977. The cast and creative contributors were:

CHARLIE CHAN .... Kirk Kirksey
WILMA .... LaTanya Richardson
PAULETTE .... Cheryl Tafathale Jones
CONSUELO .... Socorro Santiago
MATTIE .... Nikki Coleman
MIDGE .... Terria Joseph
HEAD NURSE JACOBS .... Rosanna Carter
CHARLES PAKER JR .... Arthur Burghardt
PASHA .... Le Clanché Du Rand

Director .... Bill Duke
Stage design .... Linda Conaway
Costumes .... Judy Dearing
Lighting .... Curt Osterman
Musical direction .... Dona Summers
Musicians ..... Sam Burtis, Al Harewood, Dona Summers,
Christopher White

UNFINISHED WOMEN CRY IN NO MAN'S LAND WHILE A BIRD DIES IN A GILDED CAGE

Aishah Rahman

BROADWAY PLAY PUBLISHING INC
224 E 62nd St, NY, NY 10065
www.broadwayplaypub.com
info@broadwayplaypub.com

UNFINISHED WOMEN CRY IN NO MAN'S LAND
WHILE A BIRD DIES IN A GILDED CAGE
© Copyright 1996 by Aishah Rahman

First published by B P P I in February 1997 in the collection *Plays By Aishah Rahman*
First printing this edition: December 2011
I S B N: 978-0-88145-489-5

Book design: Marie Donovan
Page make-up: Adobe Indesign
Typeface: Palatino
Printed and bound in the U S A

PLAYWRIGHT'S NOTES

Stylistically, the presentation of this play should be
in keeping with Charlie Parker's music. Bird was a
genius at improvisation, and harmonically he would
superimpose on certain fundamental notes which
created polytones. Rhythmically, he would create
an opposition of on- and off-beat accentuations and
obtain the effect of two streams of rhythms called
polyrhythms. Likewise, two streams of consciousness
is what I'm aiming for here. The two settings—
Hide-a-Wee Home for Unwed Mothers and Pasha's
boudoir— should be interplayed and intraplayed with
the dramatic image of Bird and Bird's music being
the fundamental notes that both parts bounce off on
creating tensions between them, while at the same time
weaving the seemingly disconnected parts into one
"polydrama".

Although a real musician is used as a metaphor, the
real is only a takeoff point for imagination, so please,
no imitations of Charlie Parker. The actor who plays
Parker should never put a sax to his lips. A saxophone
player offstage who is never seen must play all the
sax music. In order to sustain the metaphor of birth
and art, Consuelo's baby's cry must always be a note
from the sax. It is important to note that tape will not
substitute for live music because of the urgency and
constant playing required of the musician.

CHARACTERS & SETTING

CHARLIE CHAN, *master of ceremony*
WILMA
PAULETTE
CONSUELO
MATTIE
MIDGE
HEAD NURSE JACOBS
CHARLES PARKER, JR, *musician*
PASHA, a *European lady*

All the girls except CONSUELO *are in the last stages of pregnancy.*

Time: 1955

Place: Hide-a-Wee Home for Unwed Mothers & PASHA*'s boudoir*

For
Yoruba
All poems
All moving up

Overture

(A set that represents Hide-a-Wee Home for Unwed Mothers and PASHA's *boudoir. The underlying theme is stark vs. lush and plush. It is an old mansion that is now used as a haven for unwed mothers. Some touches of past grandeur— an ornate chandelier, perhaps a grandfather clock which never works and has to be manually adjusted to the correct time. Top floors contain the girls' rooms. Ground floor is the living room. The house contains a circular staircase. At extreme right is a balcony which is the entrance and exit to* PASHA's *boudoir, a lush, fragrant love bower.)*

(At rise: The girls are silhouetted in their rooms. PARKER *and* PASHA *are silhouetted in the boudoir.* CHARLIE CHAN *enters. He is a black man in blackface, a minstrel who acts as master of ceremony, commenting between the scenes, always remaining outside of the drama. He is a magic mimetic man. Because he is* PARKER's *alter ego, he should be dressed exactly like* PARKER *except where* PARKER *is impeccably dressed,* CHAN *is ill-fitted and tattered. He is wearing a tattered tuxedo, homburg, and white gloves.)*

CHARLIE CHAN: Ladies and gentlemen... Presenting... *Unfinished Women Cry in No Man's Land While a Bird Dies in a Gilded Cage...* A Polydrama. Dramatis personae...The Innocents...Wilma...A Black gal in conflict...Paulette...Who is Upward Bound... Consuelo...A Castilian Puerto Rican...Mattie...A Victim...Midge...All-American...Head Nurse Jacobs... Charles Parker, Jr, A great musician, and his Pasha...A rich European Lady and...yours truly, Charlie Chan,

the Invisible Man. Ladies and gentlemen, for your
entertainment... A song of mourning:
Charlie Parker done died today
Charlie Parker done died today
Charlie Parker done died today
(Piano begins to play a lush romantic tune.) Lovely tune,
isn't it?
Let's return to a memory. Think of time as a circle
going round
and round, beginning at this place or any other place
where we think we began. Where is the past? Up?
Down? I wish to relate to you the circumstances of
Birth, Death, Musicians, and Women on the day that
Charlie Parker died. Memory is *not* spontaneous. It is
the mind, rooting the soul for self-forgiveness. While
they are in this place...
this home for unwed mothers...listening to Bird's
music, being touched by his sound without
understanding the man behind the music...without
understanding any man because they are from a female
world where men are frightening and fascinating,
shadowy and intangible, not to be understood, only
loved, Bird is dying...no, not dying, but disintegrating
into pure sound...breaking open the shell of life that
contained him. Time...8:45 A M March 12, 1955.
Place...Hide-A-Wee Home for Unwed Mothers and
Pasha's boudoir. What is the connection between the
two events? Simply that it all happened at the same
moment. Time stands still. It is only we who are driven
in distorted circles and only those of us who have
chewed water know it has bones!

ENTIRE CAST: So part of what I offer you is Fantasy
And part of what I offer you is true
Which is which
Which is which
Is up to you!

Scene One

(Hide-a-Wee Home for Unwed Mothers. CHAN is an ever-present hovering spirit, reacting to the interplay of characters even though he is invisible to them. He is fixing the hands of the broken grandfather clock as NURSE JACOBS enters).

NURSE JACOBS: *(Singing)* Foolish women, wake up!
Don't you know what day this is?
What are you...deaf in one ear and can't hear out the other?
Don't you know nothing comes to a sleeper but a dream?
Better wake up and stop dreaming about the men
Who cast their love like a net, trapped you, and disappeared!

(The girls sleepily emerge from their rooms.)

MIDGE: Why all this noise in the middle of the night? I'm in a loon house. If I stay here any longer, I'll go out of my mind.

NURSE JACOBS: Oh pardon... How rude of me to interfere with Mademoiselle's repose but let me remind Her Highness that she is not at a ritzy resort but at Hide-a-Wee Home for Unwed Mothers and that it's time to wake up, wash down, and weigh in.

MIDGE: Oh well, a home is not a haven I always say...or even a peaceful hideout.

NURSE JACOBS: *(Taking a head count...dispensing towels, etc)* Where is Mattie? She still with us? Nobody went over during the night.
Did they?

MIDGE: That's right. Nobody's water broke...no babies murdered into this world. What a dull night!

(A thin, wailing, mournful cry like a baby's is played on the sax.)

WILMA: Just a crying baby who never sleeps. *(Pokes* CONSUELO*)* Hey, Connie.

CONSUELO: I told you and I told you.... My name is not Connie. It is Consuelo. Consuelo Maria Maldonando Harris.

WILMA: Harris? Since when the Harris?

CONSUELO: That's what it will be when my boyfriend comes. We're going to get married.

WILMA: I tell you, Jim, the bed is the great equalizer. Don't you know the black boys and the white boys all hand out the same shit. All right. All right. "Consuelo Maria Maldonando when-my- boyfriend-comes-we're- going-to-get-married Harris." How come I have to have the room next to you...the only girl in the house with a baby.... Can't you do something about that baby of yours hollering all night long.... God! I HATE babies!

NURSE JACOBS: Wilma!

WILMA: I mean I hate the noise they make.

CONSUELO: You won't have to worry about me much longer. My boyfriend is coming for me and the baby today and we're leaving!

PAULETTE: Ha! I hope he does come...I really do....

WILMA: Hey...did anyone hear the news? Charlie Parker died today.

NURSE JACOBS: You have serious things to think about. Today is the day. The day when you have to make a decision about what to do with them babies. So...

PAULETTE: *(Singing)* Do you really think you have to remind us what today is?
Just in case you haven't heard
There is a world outside this dump!

Ever since I been in college, I been listening to jazz!
Eric Dolphy, M J Q,
And my boyfriend who is going to be a lawyer
Listen to Charlie Parker all the time!

WILMA: *(Mimicking)* "My boyfriend is going to be a
lawyer and he listens to Charlie Parker all the time." I
always knew you were an asshole.

PAULETTE: Now you just wait a minute...

*(MATTIE slowly emerges from her room. She is younger than
the rest but she is tougher. She pops gum, rolls her eyes, and
is generally "bad." She shifts between saccharin sweetness
and quick-as-a-flash anger, but the hostility and toughness
are always underneath).*

MATTIE: Good morning, everybody.

ALL THE GIRLS: *(Mocking her)* "Good morning,
everybody!"

MATTIE: *(Hissing at them)* Shit! Godamn shit. *(Walks over
to NURSE JACOBS and sulks)*

WILMA: Hey, Paulette, honey...what you doing in a
place like this, huh? Slumming? I thought college
queens like you didn't get caught.

PAULETTE: Sugar, I know my brains and looks are a
threat to you.
I understand the hostility your type feels towards me,
but let's try to get along!

WILMA: Aw, love...you know...your daddy likes my
type. Who you think I got inside this belly. It's your
brother, bitch!

ALL THE GIRLS: OooooooOOOOO! I wouldn't take
that!

NURSE JACOBS: Stop it.... Stop it, I say.

MATTIE: Don't start again. I don't like it when you
fight!

WILMA: Look, Mattie. I'm jumpy today. Don't you know what's happening? Don't you know what day it is?

MATTIE: Of course I do. What do you think, I'm crazy? Still...I like it here.

NURSE JACOBS: Poor lamb...it was against her will...at least her conscience is clear.

PAULETTE: Her conscience may be clear but her belly isn't. It's full of a baby just like the rest of us.

NURSE JACOBS: It's not the same...the rest of you consciously sinned.

MIDGE: Love, Nurse Jacobs, is not a sin.... It's the most religious act there is.

NURSE JACOBS: Not in my church.... You're only supposed to do it to get a family. It's a sin to do it for fun and now you all have this sin on your records.

CONSUELO: I'm telling them I'm keeping my baby. Just like our Holy Virgin...Jesus's mother did.

NURSE JACOBS: Watch it about Jesus... He's only trying to teach you girls a lesson.

WILMA: *(To* CONSUELO*)* The only reason why you want your baby is because he looks white like his father and not like a Puerto Rican which is what you are!

CONSUELO: *(Singing)*
I tol' you, my mother is from Puerto Rico
But my father, he is from Spain.
He is Castilian from Madrid.
And you don't know how *Spanish* people are.
My father, he will kill him if he doesn't marry me.
Because he was the first.
My father, he knows I was a virgin!

MIDGE: It was the first time for all of us. The first time we got caught. That's why we're in this place. They only allow you one mistake. They don't let you back in here a second time.

MATTIE: What are we going to do? What are we going to tell them today? When we go downstairs what are we going to do? What are we going to tell them?

MIDGE: Hey hey hey! This day is just like any other to me. I think I'll play a set of tennis in the morning... lunch on the Riviera in the afternoon and dance a wild flamenco in Spain this evening. Oh...I don't know...to tell you the truth I haven't thought much about it.

WILMA: *(To* MIDGE*)* You don't have to give yours up.

MIDGE: I told you, I don't know.

PAULETTE: Oh Midge, you'll probably sign adoption papers today. White girls always do.

MIDGE: Oh...I don't know about all that.

WILMA: *(To* PAULETTE*)* So what.... You're planning to do the same thing.... Give up your baby... Does that make you a white girl too?

PAULETTE: All right...get off my back.

WILMA: I'm just trying to understand how you can be so calm about it...

PAULETTE: I see your kind every day, shuffling down the street in bobby sox and a two-piece maternity dress, pushing a baby carriage in one hand and a can of beer in the other. My mind is made up. Nobody knows I'm here and no one will ever know. When I leave here it will be just like this place never happened to me and if we should meet on the street just remember to pass me by!

WILMA: What's his name?

PAULETTE: Who?

WILMA: Your lawyer dude...the one who digs on
Charlie Parker.... Your F O B. Your Father of Baby?

PAULETTE: His name is Mind Your Own Business.

WILMA: Aw come on...don't hide it...divide it.... Tell us
his name.... We're all in the same boat paddling down
the same river so—

PAULETTE: I could never be like you. You have no class.

WILMA: Pregnant whore.

PAULETTE: Knocked-up cow!

WILMA: *(Going toward* PAULETTE *menacingly)* Ain't you
a bodacious bitch... Break bad if...

CONSUELO: *(Yelling over their voices)* I CAN'T hear
ANYTHING! *(Then very softly)* My baby is upstairs.
I have to listen in case he cries for me...and with all
this noise I won't be able to hear when his father
comes for me.... I can't hear if he rings the door bell
or the telephone...or he might stand outside and call
"Consuelllllooooooo, I'm here."

CHARLIE CHAN: *(From the shadows)* The music world is
still in a state of shock as the news of Charlie Parker's
death spread like wildfire. Many of Parker's friends
refused to believe it, saying it was only another wild
rumor being spread about the legendary Bird.

WILMA: *(Putting her arms around* CONSUELO) Damn you,
Charlie Parker.... Today I need you much more than
I need your music...I was with you when you walked
into oceans with your clothes on.... I wrote love letters
to myself and signed them "Bird" and even though I
love your music.... It's you...the MAN that I need.
YOU HEAR ME, CHARLIE PARKER...WE NEED
YOU!

Scene Two

(PASHA's boudoir. *The omnipresent* CHAN *steps out of the shadows and busies himself setting flowers, dusting, and generally setting the scene as* PARKER *enters upstage. He is intense, a tightly strung instrument, taut and vibrating constantly. There is enough passion in him to give one the feeling of overwhelming strength. Yet his eyes reveal a tender man...his physical aura one of intense fire that is burning out. Both bombastic and inward, low-down, funky yet poetical, intellectual, he has come to* PASHA's *boudoir to die.* PARKER *enters, looks at* PASHA, *lies on her bed without removing his shoes.* PASHA *is seated, busily tatting. She is old, or better yet, ageless. She is sinister and has a hint of past sensuousness. She is out looking in an old European-rich way. One feels the wildness within her which constantly threatens to consume her.*)

PASHA: *Ce jardin est rempli de mémoires*
Tu m'as marqué avec des piqúres
Comme une abeille passionée qui pique
On dit que tu sois un scorpion de miel

CHARLIE CHAN: This garden is full of memories
You have left bites on me
Like a stinging scorpion of passion

PARKER: They say you are a honey bee
Sticking to the flower until it is sucked dry.

PASHA: *(Turning to him, angrily)* Charles, I have wasted my youth, wondering where you are. I sent my servant scouring the city, seaching for you, combing the streets. I have been reduced to leaving messages for you in clubs.

(PARKER *is silently picking a flower from her hair and eating it.*)

PASHA: *(Laughing gaily)* I see what kind of day this will be.

Let's celebrate. We have gin and Bartók...what else do we need?

(Music: A Bartók chorale ever so lightly underneath)

CHAN/PARKER: Do you see someone?

PASHA: I have these godawful nights.... I am lonely at night without you. Let the night get some rest.... I know...we'll celebrate
(Drinking the gin glass empty) This empty glass of gin....
O! thou round and fragile goblet
Thou are more beautiful
Than the gin you once contained.

(PARKER attempts to slap PASHA; she recoils from him, protecting her face coquettishly.)

PASHA: Nooooo. It's crystal...been in the family for generations. Are you going to beat me? You're so melodramatic. None of the shadings, the subtleties for you. The trouble with you, my flamboyant, intriguing, devilish madman, is that you never want to sleep. You really must take care of yourself.

PARKER: Zookeeper, I am me. I drink too much, smoke too much, dope too much, fuck too much. Women, that is. I can't stand the smell of me.

PASHA: Where's your wife?

CHARLIE CHAN: *(Answering for PARKER)* She couldn't take it.... She went off.

PASHA: Off where?

PARKER: How the fuck am I supposed to know? She just evaporated like all frail things. Get out!

PASHA: *(Realizing he is ill, going toward him)* Lie down, baby, I'll call my doctor.

PARKER: *(Pushes her away)* Why? Does he know where my wife is?
I didn't send for you. Get the fuck out of my house.

PASHA: *(Resuming tatting)* I ain't leaving. I live here... remember? Lace.... I'm weaving some lace and then I'll fashion a handkerchief from it. After all, every gentleman of color should have a lace mouchoir.

PARKER: *(Caught in a spasm of violent coughing)* Damn! I sure used up this motherfucker. I might not make the gig.

(PASHA goes toward him again. He pushes her away.)

PARKER: No, please. I came here because you're good for me. You give me what I need and some of what I don't.

(PASHA begins to sway and dance seductively for him. PARKER continues.)

PARKER: You are so relaxed, so cool. I like your looseness. It must come from being rich.

PASHA: *(Still dancing)* Did you know that there aren't too many women who are into jazz. All they want to know is money. But if a man is a serious-minded musician...he's got to have time and space to think... and he needs a woman like me...don't you agree?

PARKER: Fuck you, Pasha! I want a glass of gin!

(PASHA slowly pours a drink and offers it to PARKER. He looks at the drink a long time and slowly pushes her hand away. She immediately understands that it is more than a rejection of the drink but of herself. She furiously takes up her tatting.)

PASHA: Our child...I'll make us our child.

PARKER: PASHA!

PASHA: Here's the head...two holes for the eyes....

PARKER: Stop it!

PASHA: *(Tatting furiously)* Some lungs. Lungs for our child to breathe.

(PARKER *lunges toward her tatting;* PASHA *swiftly moves it deftly out of his reach.*)

PASHA: No! I will not let you kill this one!

PARKER: You're a witch!

PASHA: (*Holding the tatting, caressing it*) It's my baby. My dream. The child that I want. I will make it come true.

PARKER: You are evil.

PASHA: I'm not evil. Why am I left alone night after night like some dried-up tree? We could have a child if you would touch me and hold me. Why don't you treat me like a woman?

PARKER: (*Slowly going toward her*) Oh for God's sake. Not now...please...it's much too late. I came here because I need a friend. Nooo, you are much more than that. I came here because I need someone...who loves me and that's all. No needs. Just love... You do love me, don't you? Pasha... Don't destroy me with whatever I happen to leave laying around of myself.

PASHA: (*Slowly dropping her tatting to the floor*) Charles.... Don't be foolish.

Scene Three

(*Hide-a-Wee. All the girls are gathered for daily examination.*)

NURSE JACOBS: (*Examining* MATTIE) Just what I suspected! You're gaining too much weight. Too much salt. Lord, today.... You're swollen and probably toxic.

PAULETTE: I told you not to eat that whole jar of pickles.

MATTIE: I like 'em.

(*All the girls laugh uproariously.*)

NURSE JACOBS: You think it's funny, don't you. You think it's funny if she gorges herself with salt and swells up like a balloon. All right. Everybody off salt.

ALL THE GIRLS: What!

NURSE JACOBS: No more salt on the table. No salt in the crackers. No salt in the ocean and no salt in your tears. No more salt, I say! Don't you know it's a mortal sin if you harm your babies?

CONSUELO: Ay, ay, ay...no salt...just because of one person?

NURSE JACOBS: You are your sister's keeper. Especially Mattie.

WILMA: Don't let Mattie fool you. She can take care of herself.

(MATTIE *laughs*.)

NURSE JACOBS: Mattie isn't the only one. After I gave strict orders for your diets, I've seen you sneak french fries and salted peanuts. I think you are purposely trying to cross God by harming your babies.... No salt for anyone, I say.... Now! You see the shame and burden loose ways bring upon a girl...it don't pay to be worthless!

ALL THE GIRLS: (*Chanting and dancing mockingly*)
I got it.
It's in my bed.
A loaf of bread.
I got it.
It's in my stomach.
I want to vomit.
I got it.
You know I got it.
It's in my booty.
Tutti frutti!

NURSE JACOBS: Stop it. Stop this nastiness, I say!

WILMA: Nurse J... Is it true you still a virgin?

(General laughter)

NURSE JACOBS: Is a rudeness you have, talking to me so. Dog my age ain't no pup, you know.

WILMA: I was just wondering if you made of stone... that's all. No offense.

NURSE JACOBS: I ain't studying myself with the niggers of this world. Besides, I have God and my Bible!

WILMA: You still a woman...and a human being. Every human has feelings. Every woman is flesh.

NURSE JACOBS: See what your flesh and feeling reaped. It ain't *me* having to hide away shame to face people. Now hear me right. I ain't saying I ain't not looking for someone suitable. When I finish raising up my niece I hoping to meet some nice retired old gentleman with a nice pension who ain't looking for bed companion and want someone to fetch him a glass of water in his old age. Perhaps me and him could come to an understanding....

(All the girls laugh.)

NURSE JACOBS: Shhh, hurry up, hurry up. Time is flying and fate will not be kept waiting today. You all know what has to be done. Papers have to be signed. Adoption forms have to be filled out.

CONSUELO: No!

NURSE JACOBS: Look...I just trying to do my job. You from this country, you don't understand. Back home there ain't nothing to do. Here, I take up nurse aid and graduate to head nurse. I happy to be working in this country and I just trying to do my job. So hurry up!

MATTIE: Admit it, Nurse Jacobs...you hate all of us.

NURSE JACOBS: Not so, precious lamb. That ain't the truth at all. Don't you know I think of you all as my own daughters?

MATTIE: I don't know nothing except this baby is in my belly and gonna come out my pussy with blood and piss and shit. I'm scared.

MIDGE: Nothing to it, sugar, nothing to it. We're just wonderful vessels of creation for the Lord!

(Suddenly the wailing cry of the sax)

CONSUELO: My baby!

NURSE JACOBS: Your baby's awake again, Consuelo...go see to your son. I bet he knows the seriousness of this day.

(Girls and CONSUELO laugh defiantly.)

NURSE JACOBS: Laugh, go ahead...but remember...God is strict, very strict. And before this day is over, I bet you all gonna be laughing on the other side of your faces.

Scene Four

(NURSE JACOBS is alone onstage. She speaks to the audience.)

NURSE JACOBS: I been through this day a hundred times...watching hundreds of girls go downstairs and make their decisions to give up their babies or...whatever. And I still can't...still can't help remembering. Yes! I had a man once. Is Gospel! He broke holes in the air with his laughter! Big-time Calypsonian. Playing from island to island. He, writing me all the time these love letters: "Darlin'...I lonely for you. Your heart in front of my eyes all the time. Take care of our green baby growin' inside of you, sweetheart. I missing you in that certain way." Sweet,

sweet words. I getting bigger and bigger and happier
and happier. I didn't have no shame then, only love.
I getting ready the marrying things, the white dress,
veil, even the eats and drinks and then...nothing...no
sweet words...no promises...
nothing. Nothing slowly stretches into nothing. Savior
in heaven...
you forgive Mary Magdalene so why not me? I paid
my penance for my hour of passion. I work hard...
keep man outta my life and raise my...my..."niece"
(Angrily) Yes...yes...I calling me own *daughter* my
niece. You don't understand. Back home we dont have
places like this. A girl in trouble has to make her own
arrangements. I went to another island...bought myself
a wedding ring and gave birth to
my "niece". It's been hard...all these years...keeping my
daughter a secret...raising up me "niece" by myself...
but I hanging on.... Praise God.... I hanging on!

Scene Five

(PASHA's *boudoir. As usual* CHAN *watches in the shadows,
only emerging to play the servant.*)

PASHA: There is no force like desire. It gets rooted in
the blood and runs wild. Burning you up! I want my
youth.... My youth, Parker... I'll tat my youth again...
then you will look at your Pasha...with desire.

PARKER: I dreamed of a giant bird with wings so big
they spread out against the sky and blocked out the
sun. The bird had a man's face and was really half God
and half Man with wings. But the two halves were
fighting each other to death. Biting and killing each
other right there in the middle of space...screeeching
across the bleeding sky. And it was only when the bird,
Man-God, the whole thing when it would fall to earth

and be born again as an ordinary person...only then would the sun be able to shine again.

PASHA: Do you ever dream of me?

PARKER: I don't know, Pasha, maybe.... But I dream that I am a musician, with money, power, luxury that I earned because of my great music without a boss... without anyone to make fun of me or bring me down.... I give you my dreams as a gift.

(PASHA *holds a golden spoon of drugs under his nose.*)

PARKER: Tat me a womb, Pasha...not attached to anybody...just some unattached place for me to lay my head. You can do it. You can do anything....

PASHA: (*Sarcastically*) You mean...I can give you anything.

PARKER: Yes, you are rich.

PASHA: Yes, I am rich. And wallowing in poverty. Give me a child.

(PARKER *takes the golden spoon.* PASHA *knocks it from his hand.*)

PASHA: I'm sick of drugs, booze, jazz, all of it. I'm a WOMAN.

PARKER: GET AWAY!

PASHA: Don't push me away.... LOVE ME.

PARKER: (*Knocking her down*) BLOODSUCKER! Get the hell away from me!

PASHA: Nigger! You owe me something! I've invested everything I believe in you!

PARKER: You. You don't love me.... You want to use me. You want to own me! You want to control me. You want to destroy me.

PASHA: Destroy you? Me? Uh-uh, baby. I'm the one that always bails you out. I'm the one that saves your ass! You the one. Don't pull that shit on me. You are the dude that wants to die and is always busy killing himself. I want you to live.

PARKER: *(Laughing sarcastically)* I can dig it...but don't you worry about me killing myself. I'm merely on a path to the sublime... But what would you know about that... You're not a musician... You are just a shell... waiting to be filled up.... *(Falls back, exhausted)*

PASHA: *(Cradling his head)* Waiting...yes, waiting to be filled by you. What's so wrong about that? Just because I want to be a part of you and your music...a part of its creation. Don't put me down. Please.

PARKER: I want to separate myself from you and all that ties me to this earth. There is one perfect note. Too perfect for human ears.
Yet, *I* keep on hearing it all the time. And when I do every cell of
my body wants to break up into tiny parts of that one perfect musical note and float on the ear of every living soul. WHAT A SONG. WHAT A PERFECT COSMIC MELODY I WOULD BE AT THAT MOMENT! Goddamn. GET ME MY DRUGS!

PASHA: Why do you put so much effort into being insane?

PARKER: We don't understand each other. We belong in two different worlds.

PASHA: But we're both trapped in this one so would you try not to hate me so much?

PARKER: Me? I love you.

PASHA: You're making fun of me.

PARKER: It's true...I do.... I love your passion for jazz...a language you don't understand.

PASHA: I don't understand? Really, Bird.... Sometimes you talk to me as if I'm unintelligent.

PARKER: *(Slowly, as if teaching a child)* It's not a question of intelligence. It's a matter of feeling. Of being able to operate *in*
things and not *from* things. I'm trying to communicate *feelings*, baby, not knowledge.

PASHA: *(Shaking her head in agreement)* I understand.

PARKER: Do you? Do you really? Who are you? Who do you think I am?

PASHA: Who am I? I am the farmer. You are the seed. I am the farmer that nurtures the seed. You are the genius but I am the power.

PARKER: You...are...a ho...baby, that's all. Clear and simple. A ho.

PASHA: *(Matter-of-factly correcting his pronunciation)* A whore...not ho. *(Spelling it out)* W-H-O-R-E!

(They both laugh.)

PARKER: When a man loves a woman, he may beat on her, pee on her, adore her, spit on her, cry at the sight of her, torture her, kiss all her toes. When a woman loves a man, she simply wants to become his whore.

PASHA: Why do I have to be whore or saint? Can't I just be ordinary?

PARKER: You're right. You can afford to be ordinary.

PASHA: Damn right, I'm ordinary. Most of my life has been spent doing nothing and being generally in the way. I was bored before. *(Throwing back her head laughing)* Did you know that my family owned the original land grant to Manhattan?

PARKER: You mean the Indians? Damn!

PASHA: You see, Darling. We're made for each other. You're a legend. So am I.

CHAN/PARKER: *(In unison)* As one legend said to the other: Shut up and let's get high.

Scene Six

(Hide-a-Wee. WILMA *enters. She is alone.)*

WILMA: *(To audience)* You know, I first dug Bird 'cause everybody was into him and used to talk about him all the time. Then when I really listened to him.... Dudes 'round my way would only take their special woman to dig Bird with. I went down to Birdland one night and everybody was waiting for him and when he finally showed he looked like he slept under the bandstand and hadn't shaved for weeks. I never saw anything like that and I never heard anything like his music. Charlie Parker played in tongues... I don't want to give up my baby, but I know that it's a boy in here. Funny what Bird means to me. Secretly, I always wanted to be a man 'cause they can do things and go places. Bird is the man I wanted to be. Maybe my son will be like him. Dig that. Maybe I'm giving up a Charlie Parker. Maybe I'm thinking about giving up a Charlie Parker. The baby's father? He's just someone I met at a dance. Tall, dark, and good-looking. And I like the way his smile tasted in my mouth. Anthony. He smiled at me and I smiled back and we wanted each other.He's just a man I gave myself to and I can't blame him for anything. Really. But I do because I'm here and he's... *(Shrugging her shoulders helplessly)* You know what this is? *(Puts her hand on her stomach)* It's a curse... it got my mother and now it's got me...fatherless child, manless woman, it's deep, it's always there waiting, no matter how you try to escape. I watched it pick us off like typhoid, one by one. We knew a girl had caught it when her belly got bigger and bigger and her eyes took on a certain feverish look and everybody wondered who's next...who's next...and now it's my turn....

(Music up)

WILMA: In Anthony's room, in his bed, lying there on my back, I could feel myself far below him, I was on the bottom of an ocean and he was the moon way up over me. A moon I could smell, a moon I could touch but whose face floated in and out of my mind. His body was spread all over, covering me like space. I crouched inside of myself, listening like an animal to our silence. Then, very faint at first...the sound of Bird's horn...tugging at me, taking me back to a memory I was born with. Following the music's heartbeat I took a journey I could no longer avoid and along the way I helped a woman toss her newborn baby overboard a slaveship. I joined hands with my mother as she took her mother's hand and I took my place in the circle of black women singing old blues. The man, spread high above me, worked over me, his sweat dripping down in my eyes and my voice screaming higher and higher along with Parker's sax...both sounds pouring over me, pulling me, pushing me to a point of passion, a point of pain and then...silence...and the smell of rain falling outside as he breaks into my womb and bursts inside of me, overflowing on the sheets and bed and everything and I knew that the cycle of passion and pain, blood and birth, and aloneness had once again started, inside of me, and I lay there wondering how many moons before I could become virgin again!

(Music up as she listens for a few beats)

WILMA: Hear that? He's not dead. Bird lives.... Inside here. *(Embracing her stomach)* Bird's alive.... Oh yes, he's alive. *(Bursting into song)*
O lovely music man

Women want you for your energy.
Many love you for your song.
The whole universe
Swings to your melodies.
And everybody will listen
When I shout.... Bird Lives, Bird Lives, Bird Lives!

Scene Seven

(Hide-a-Wee. All the girls are present except WILMA. *They
are clowning it up.)*

ALL THE GIRLS: *(Chanting a 1950s hit)*
Earth Angel, Earth Angel
Will you be mine.
My darlin' dear
Love you all the time.
I'm just a fool
Just a fool in love.

MIDGE: All right, all right... It's your roving reporter.
Tell me, dear. How did you happen to get here?

MATTIE: *(Speaking seductively, like a whore talking to a
prospective john)* Pssst! Come here.... I was framed...
know what I mean...I really was. I did it to *(Counting
fast on her fingers)* ten boys including my brother and
first cousin and had been in love with all of them, you
know what I mean. Then one night I ate this really
sweet red juicy watermelon...know what I mean? But
I swallowed some seeds by mistake...you know how
you do when you eat watermelon and it's so good and
cold and juicy you just want to swallow it and you
don't have time to separate the seeds from the juice so I
just swallowed it all and the next morning I awake and
pfffft...just like that.... That's why you should always
chew your food and spit out the seeds and bones and
things like that. Know what I mean?

MIDGE: I said my name is Purity and I am twin sister to the Virgin Mary. I too have been visited by a holy ghost and I shall bring forth a son which shall be called UNBELIEVABLE.

(All laugh as NURSE JACOBS enters.)

NURSE JACOBS: Would you look at this. I don't believe my two eyeholes. Time done run out and you still cutting the fool.

(Music: a long lone cry on the saxophone as NURSE JACOBS continues)

NURSE JACOBS: Consuelo...go to your room. Your baby needs changing. Wilma! Paulette! You better go watch Consuelo so you
can learn how to be mothers.

PAULETTE: *(Yelling offstage)* I am not going to be a mother. I'm not even going to see my baby.

NURSE JACOBS: You all will see your babies. Maybe now you realize this ain't no joke— ha! *(She exits.)*

MIDGE: None of us has to be here...I mean we all could be on the outside now.... So we got caught.... Why didn't we get rid of it?
I mean...why didn't any of us have an abortion?

(Meanwhile, the sax has become more insistent as if to pull CONSUELO upstairs. She slowly works her way toward the exit while talking.)

CONSUELO: Shh! Don't say such a thing. Don't you know it's a sin even to talk that way?

MATTIE: My social worker said the State would get me one if I could prove I was raped like I said. Shit! How can I prove that?

CONSUELO: I'd rather go through all this than die on some butcher's table or go to jail. Besides, where would I get the money for one anyhow?

MIDGE: I guess underneath I was saying to myself: If I can't have him.... *(Shrugs her shoulders without completing her sentence. Trying to change the mood, she sings the following.)*
Beware of young men
in their velvet prime
who give so little
and take so much
and make a girl old
before her time.
Those gay young men
in their velvet prime.

(They laugh as if it is a big joke on themselves. CONSUELO *has almost exited and then she rushes back.)*

CONSUELO: I am not here.... No.... You think you see me, but I am not here. I am in the lovely island of Puerto Rico...visiting relatives. Let me tell you about my sweetheart. We would love each other till we would burst out singing! Our love danced in the air for hours. And all the time...mi madre... "Casate con un hombre Americano, casate con un hombre Americano...marry an American...get something out of this life, make something for yourself." She practically made the bed for us to lie in. My poor mother...when she was young she gave away my older sister because there was no money...my sister becomes my first cousin. Then I come along, still no money. This time my father borrows money from his boss to have me aborted. They were young. It is a spring afternoon when my mother knocks the money down to the ground. Neither one of them picks it up. Now...they have to lie about me...telling people I'm in Puerto Rico. So, here I am in Puerto Rico...visiting friends.

MIDGE: I'm beginning to love Latin music. When I first got to New York a friend of mine took me down to the Palladium.

CONSUELO: Oh yeah, Tito Puente, Machito, Palmieri... the way some Spanish girls turn on the radio and listen to music all day long...the way I used to move my body from side to side and stick out my behind makes me sick. I don't like Latin music much.... Now Perry Como. I love Perry Como, don't you?

MIDGE: *(Laughing)* PERRY COMO!

CONSUELO: You're always laughing at me. Asking me questions. But you never talk about yourself, do you?

MIDGE: I hardly know myself, so how can I give anyone a chance to know me?

(Music: the cry of the sax)

CONSUELO: I'm coming. I'm coming. *(Reluctantly going toward exit and then turning back)* Lately I don't know myself either. You ever read in the newspaper about women who kill babies? I just always have to read cases like that all the way through from beginning to end. Maybe twice even. I read all the details and can't seem to draw myself away from them. I'll kill my baby— NO! I love my baby. Oh, I don't know.... He's coming, isn't he? He's coming to take me out of here, isn't he?

MIDGE: Sure, sure, you bet. He's coming.... He'll show up.

CONSUELO: But when? It's almost time to... *(Beat)* change the baby. *(She exits.)*

MATTIE: What about you— what about your F O B?

MIDGE: *(Still clowning, the following said with tongue in cheek)* The father of my baby. Well, it was the first time—

(Groans from all the girls, as PAULETTE *enters, standing silently, watching* MIDGE.*)*

MIDGE: Well, it was.... If I don't count all those times
under the stairs and in the car where everything else
happened...kissing, sucking, biting...letting a dude
in just a little bit...just the tip but not all the way....
And I don't count the times when I let a guy in but
I was too young to have my period so I couldn't get
pregnant yet.... But this night was different. There was
something inside of me overripe....
I was one big Yessssss...ready to receive him....

PAULETTE: *(Sarcastically)* Yeah...yeah...yeah...

MIDGE: *(Ignoring* PAULETTE*)* My stomach was lean and
flat.

PAULETTE: Yeah, sure, I bet.

MIDGE: Desire was my name.

PAULETTE: WHY DON'T YOU TELL THEM YOUR
F O B IS A BLACK NIGGA!

MIDGE: *(Very quietly)* Why are you yelling at me?

PAULETTE: I AM NOT YELLING!

MIDGE: Why are you angry?

PAULETTE: I am not angry.... Yes, yes, I am angry.
You'll go through this day like a breeze and still have a
privileged place waiting for *you* on the outside.

MIDGE: What privileged place? The privilege of raising
my black baby by myself. Walking down the street
with it, trying to ignore the smirks of both blacks and
whites who are offended by my mulatto bastard?
`Cause that's just what people like you will call my
baby.
Or the privilege of giving it away like it never existed?
Look at you all standing around wondering what kind
of white girl would end up in a place like this. You
think you have a monopoly on pain?
How do you think it feels to tell the man you love

you're going to have his baby and all he can say is "I'm sorry." And now he's gone. So tell me what's so privileged about that?

(PAULETTE *laughs at* MIDGE *mockingly.*)

MATTIE: But I never even had a boyfriend. Why do I have to have baby when I never even had a boyfriend?

NURSE JACOBS: (*Over a P A system*) Attention... attention...girls of Hide-a-Wee. A family from Westchester coming through to inspect the house. Those girls who don't want to be seen may return to their rooms.

MATTIE: They can kiss my ass. What do I care who sees me? I only came here because my probation officer made me. They can put my picture in the *Daily News* for all I care!

Scene Eight

(PASHA's *boudoir.* CHAN, *the omnipresent solicitous servant, is hovering about in the background as usual.* PARKER, *restless, half sings, half talks the following:*)

PARKER: Today! What a beautiful day.
Sun shining like a soft golden woman. Today!
Sun shining
like a soft golden woman
Wrapping herself around me
Wrapping herself around me.
OH! Today!
What a beautiful day.
Sun shining
Like a soft golden woman
Wrapping herself around.

PASHA: (*Hands* PARKER *a dish and a coke spoon*) It's here, in this crystal dish, Darling.

(PARKER *smiles at* PASHA, *reaches out, and then quickly withdraws his hand. Music underneath the following...light, airy jazz tune.*)

PARKER: I've found it...the unknowable why...locked up in my music. Music. My music. O god O god...the women I've known.... All they ever wanted from me was to stay out of jail...and make some money...and all I ever wanted to do was fly.... Pasha...please...you tell them that I loved them I love them....

PASHA: There's a rumor going around that you shoot dope in your dick vein.

PARKER: (*Coughing*) I am what I am...as I was shaped. I'm only sorry I only have one joint!

PASHA: (*Going toward him to help him with his spasm of coughing*)
Why don't you let me call my doctor?

PARKER: (*Summoning all his strength to push her away*)
Will you stop treating me like a dying man? Now listen. I just stopped by to tell you that I'm splitting the scene. I need to be somewhere else. I think I'll hat up and go to Italy.... Do Europe for a while.

PASHA: (*Dipping spoon in the crystal dish and sniffing coke*)
All right Charles...here's to being somewhere else.

PARKER: (*Doubling over as if in terrible pain*) KICK ME IN MY ASS! PASHA VON KWONGESTRA, I WANT YOU TO KICK ME IN MY ASS!

PASHA: (*Backing away from him, truly frightened this time*)
Naw... Noooooooooooooo

PARKER: (*Still bending over, insisting*) Right here in the crack.

PASHA: No, Bird, no.

PARKER: WOMAN! Do what I tell you. Look at me. (*Stands up suddenly and grabs her*) LOOK AT ME I SAID.

O god, LOOK AT ME! Music is my only motive....
My only alibi...for living. Clubs are named after me.
Musicians make it...imitating me. And I can't even give
it away. I stand around begging people to let me play.
I...am...Charles...Parker, Jr...and I beg people to let me
play. KICK ME, Pasha *(Bending over again)* DAMN
YOU...KICK MEEEE....

(As if jolted by his screaming, PASHA *gives him a vicious
kick that sends him sprawling on the floor. She runs to him
and kneels down on the floor, caressing him.* CHAN *wipes a
tear from his eyes.)*

PASHA: *(Caressing* PARKER *on floor, singing.)*
A musician is neither a soldier
Nor keeps a horse
Nor has a family
Yet in the pride of his ancient art
He remains discontent.

PARKER: *(Rising to his full height) C'est un grand malheur
de perdre, par notre caractère, les droits que nos talents nous
donnent sur la société.*

CHAN: Meaning...in this country...a nigger ain't shit!

PARKER: *(Making a sound of agony)* Cha!

PASHA: *(Rising)* I want you to take some money and go
someplace. Ibithia...go to Ibithia...lay up in the sun...
do the Spanish coastline. I'll call my doctor...he'll fix
up everything.... I have some friends there.... They'll
let you have a house and a boat...take somebody with
you...your wife.... I could find her and you two could
try to get your thing together....

PARKER: *(Putting his finger to her lips to stop her flow of
words)* It's all right, Baby. My pain is *not* unbearable...I
feel good. Really I do. In none of the places inside...in
none of my secret places inside me have I condemned
myself!

Scene Nine

(Hide-a-Wee Home and PASHA's *boudoir.* PARKER *and* PASHA *are in the boudoir as* PAULETTE *enters the living room of Hide-a-Wee. The voices of the characters weave in and out of one another, overlapping.)*

PAULETTE: I am not like them. I am not. I feel so different from them. Oh yes, I know we're all pregnant in here but I'm different. My family expects certain things from me.... My father...has given me everything.... I've got a family name to live up to. My mother...I used to watch my mother sitting at the dinner table listening to everybody's lives.... I grew up in my father's house and was never allowed to call him anything but "Sir." "Yes, Sir." "You do understand that cultured Negroes listen to classical music, not jazz." "Oh, yes, Sir." And now it's "You will give your baby up for adoption so you can come home and be my daughter again." You know what.... I always always felt like his victim.... Sometimes I want to keep my baby so I can be free of him...free to be what I want to be...maybe this dream I keep having would stop haunting me—

PARKER: Sometimes I wish I could be a thought, a sound
Anything, but flesh....

PASHA: I could be anything you let me be
Anything you need
Come be the child in my womb.... Come and be my seed.

WILMA/PAULETTE: I want to be free
Not what my body dictates to me.

PARKER: Wish milk could flow from my body
Wish I could cry my tears
Scream out my fears.

PASHA: Once I had a thousand nipples that suckled a thousand men.

PARKER: O! to be free. Not a giant, not a god, not a man!

WILMA: I could be Charlie Parker
Oh the many selves of me
If I could be free, free
To be who I want to be.

PAULETTE: *(Reaching out to touch* WILMA*)* Wilma—

WILMA: Uh-huh.

PAULETTE: Can't you see I'm trying to talk to you?

WILMA: Go ahead, nobody's stopping you.

PAULETTE: I'm, I'm only trying to...look, I had this dream, keep having this dream, and you and I are in it, so I thought— look, I know how I've acted but it's just that I can't stand the sight of
you or myself or the rest of these pregnant girls. Victims. Helpless victims. Sniveling after a man.

WILMA: What about your F O B? Your lawyer dude. Don't you want him? Don't you love him?

PAULETTE: Love? He was exciting but I don't want his baby. I want music and anisette in delicate amber glasses...caviar...not babies. Babies weigh you down, inside and outside. I bet a woman first used the word "love". And that's just what "love" is. A woman's weakness. Listen...just listen to the sounds outside.... Cars, rivers, people, all moving. Going different places. Late at night when all of you are asleep, I get up and stand by my window listening to the world. Music and feet and voices and bodies and sights and dreams and shouting mixed up together, calling me. I want to reach out and grab those sounds. I want to go! I want to live! I got visions! I want to do crazy things like walk down the Champs Élysées with a panther on a leash like Josephine Baker. But a man will stop a woman. Someway, somehow, he just manages to pump you full of babies and insecurities and turn you into a rag doll that only lives through him....

WILMA: You...make...me...sick! You have a place in this world. You could give your child anything. Everything! Me...I have nothing...to hold on to. It all gets destroyed somehow...like...like...Charlie Parker. You did it!

PAULETTE: I don't understand what you're saying.

WILMA: I know you don't. Your kind never does. That's how you killed Bird, too. By not understanding. THAT'S RIGHT, YOU AND YOUR WORLD KILLED BIRD!

PAULETTE: Don't say that. Don't ever say that. I loved him too! Bird played for everybody and I heard him too.

WILMA: I just bet you did. Charlie Parker was something we had over white folks and people like you. White boys with millionaire fathers and debutante ball niggas...pretending to be so hip. Screaming for the Bird! If you once knew, if one of you knew the pain he was playing about, you couldn't take it. Ya couldn't listen to him. Well, I knew. And I want to take your world and shake it. That's why I can't keep my baby... until I make a place for me.

PAULETTE: *(Going to her)* What are you saying?

WILMA: That I am going to give my baby up for adoption.... Maybe.

PAULETTE: Wilma!

WILMA: *(Almost as if arguing to herself)* I...said...maybe. After all. I don't have any business keeping this baby. Except that it's a part of me. I keep seeing myself in the future. Each day like a slap in the face. Each year saying to me, "Your son is one year older and you don't know where he is or who's got him or how to try to get him back." Don't look at me like that.

PAULETTE: I am not looking at you.

WILMA: After all...you don't know what you are going to do either.

PAULETTE: I do. I have definitely come to a decision.... I have decided that I can't sit back and wait for things to happen. This is the last time I will sit and wait. I'll never let this happen to me again. I don't care how many men I have to fight. I will fuck them or fight them with my bare fists. Whatever way I can hurt them best.

WILMA: Tell me.

PAULETTE: What?

WILMA: The dream. You said you had a dream....

PAULETTE: Yes...I'll tell you.

WILMA: Well, go ahead. I'm waiting.

PAULETTE: I'll try and tell you. It seems like this dream is deep deep inside of me and it comes floating to the top night after night. In this dream I am making love over and over but I can't see who the man is...his face is hidden by a mist, but I finally manage to lift the fog and behind it is the man who is my lover but only he is not a man but a woman and well I think that woman is you and I wake up when I see that and I'm ashamed and scared, promising myself never to have that dream again and yet I know it's there, in the pillows, in the sheets, waiting for me to come to bed and dream it once again.

WILMA: (*Laughing*) What do you expect. We've been in this no man's land for days, waiting and waiting. Just waiting. I'm so horny I have wet dreams even when I'm awake!

PAULETTE: But with a woman...? I'm not like that!

WILMA: It's only a dream. You don't have to be afraid. It's only a dream. You know what...sometimes I think... about...that too. Well why not? We've been used, hurt, and abandoned by our men. Is it so wrong to look for an alternative to pain even if it's only in our subconscious?

PAULETTE: What are we going to do? What are we going to do?

WILMA: *(Putting her arms around* PAULETTE*)* Right now, we're gonna have these babies. And do what we have to. And one day, I hope that we won't have to be afraid of our own dreams.

Scene Ten

*(*PASHA's *boudoir.* PARKER *is lying down, feverish.* PASHA *is wiping his brow.)*

PARKER: *(Suddenly jumping up)* I'm on...it's time for me to go on the bandstand!

PASHA: *(Struggles with him, trying to make him lie down, but he breaks free)* Lie down, you are feverish.

PARKER: GET OUT OF MY WAY. I'm on. It's time for me to go on the bandstand.

(Music: Cherokee *plays softly underneath.)*

CHARLIE CHAN: *(Stepping out of corner)* Good evening, ladies and gentlemen, and welcome to the world-famous Birdland.... Here's Charlie Parker and *Cherokee.*

*(*PASHA *begins to dance and sway and snap her fingers to the music.)*

PARKER: Hear that, my music. You know what *they* call it? "Be-bop." Yeah, that's right, "Be-bop be-bop be-bop!" How can anyone take music that's called "be-bop" seriously?

CHARLIE CHAN: Good evening, ladies and gentlemen, and welcome to the world-famous Birdland.... Here's Charlie Parker and "Cherokee."

PARKER: When I go on that bandstand
I want folks to hear me as I am
Low-down and funky
Hear me without tears
Without pity
Let them wish that they could cook like me
When I go on that bandstand
I want folks to see me as I am
Shouting and happy
See me wild
See me free
Got to go now...it's time for my solo!

CHARLIE CHAN: Good evening, ladies and gentlemen, and welcome to the world-famous Birdland.... Here's Charlie Parker and *Cherokee.*

PARKER: Nobody lives for a lifetime
I'm even wanting to go
I'm not worried about my body
I've used it, it's finished, I'm glad
All I ever waited for was the music
All the beauty there has ever been
A dog's bark, a child's cry
The voice the wind had in Africa
The intention of trees
And memories
Waiting...and suffering
Looking at the sky
It's right here...inside the music.

Scene Eleven

(Hide-a-Wee living room. All five girls are sitting and waiting. CHAN adjusts the clock, which begins to tick ominously. MATTIE gets up and puts a shawl on her shoulder, and takes a necklace from her pocket, primping as if she were going out for a stroll.)

MATTIE: *(Looks straight at audience)* I got this false I D card that says I'm eighteen. Had it made up on 42nd Street in one of those stores. And when I put on my makeup and shit I know I could pass maybe even for twenty-one. Wish I could use it now and go down to Birdland and listen to some music and have a beer or something.... That place of Momma's...not secret enough to keep their eyes and hot man smell offa me. You got to hide under the wallpaper to get safe. Were you there? I couldn't see who it was...they just pinned me down and tore off my panties...but fuck it.... I got something for you mothers. *(She whips an ice-pick from her bosom.)* Meet Foo-Foo, my best friend. Foo-Foo used to be the name of my doll I used to sleep with.... Now I sleep with this here Foo-Foo...anybody come near me.... WHOOOSH! *(She stabs an invisible assailant.)* I don't want a son-of-a-bitch to even look like he gone ask me for some pussy much less take it...I....

CONSUELO: Okay sugar...take off my shawl...and give me that.

PAULETTE: You better put that away before you hurt yourself. Aw, baby...not my necklace...didn't I tell you to stay out of my suitcase?

MATTIE: Are you referring to these old things.... My boyfriends gave `em to me, nice, huh? *(Then suddenly angry, throws things at them)* Here, take your shit.... Here, you take your shit too.

CONSUELO: Oh, Mattie...the ice pick...give us the ice pick.

PAULETTE: *(Holding out the necklace to* MATTIE*)* You can have it...if you let me have the ice pick. Here girl, wear them...they are yours.... I was only kidding.

MATTIE: *(Backing away from them)* No....no, don't touch.... Don't give me anything.

*(*PAULETTE *and* CONSUELO *go to* MATTIE *and hug her.* MATTIE *drops the ice pick to the floor.)*

MATTIE: I mean, what would I do with a gift...anyhow?

Scene Twelve

(Hide-a-Wee and PASHA's *boudoir. All characters are onstage. The structure of this scene is nearest to a spontaneous jazz piece. Free-form saxophone music dominates and is played steadily throughout, sometimes underneath, sometimes up front, but always there. The entire drama bursts into music and voices. The characters repeat the following dialogue over and over, weaving in and out of, on top and below, each other, accelerating in pace, volume and intensity.* CHAN *opens the scene by fixing the clock. As the scene grows,* CHAN *jerks and twists in agony, his frantic body movements almost in time to the music, as if he has internalized everybody's pain.)*

NURSE JACOBS: *(Watching* CHAN *fix clock)* It's time!

PAULETTE: No...it is not time...already...it couldn't be.

(The saxophone plays a refrain over and over.)

WILMA: *(Hugging her stomach and rocking)* It's only in the head of a musician that I begin to understand. Only a musician can make sense for me. Only a musician knows how to connect shoes with cardboard to cover holes to P S 184 on 116th Street and Lenox Avenue to the red taste of watermelon and mocking white smiles to Anthony's smile and smell of Florida Water to late-night loneliness and...this....

NURSE JACOBS: You have all made a mistake and now is the time to correct it.

CONSUELO: He's not coming, is he? Tell my mother he's not coming.

MIDGE: This place is the only place—

NURSE JACOBS: And of your own free will—

MATTIE: Why do I have to have a baby?

WILMA: Oooooweeeeeeeeee the pain...it hurts—

MIDGE: This place is the only place—

PAULETTE: DADDY!

CONSUELO: Mother...he's not coming, he's not here.

PARKER: Breakingintobreakingintobreakingintobreakinginto-breakingintobreakingintothe songthe songthe songthe song-breaking intothe songthe songthe song.

PASHA: Once...I had a thousand nipples—

NURSE JACOBS: Relinquish your child foreverrelinquishyourchild forever—

WILMA: I'm pushing! It's coming! I need you! Need, need, need.

PARKER: You hear it? The songthesongsongsong youheritthe songthesongsongsongsong?

MATTIE: (To audience) Listen, you think I could come and cook for you sometime? I could make hot dogs and chili and you could be my boyfriend. Please, huh? Not now...I mean later...after....

NURSE JACOBS: Who is keeping her baby and who is giving it away?

PAULETTE: There is no way of preparing for this. You know it's coming and you think about it all the time but there is no way of getting ready.

NURSE JACOBS: (*Raising her hand as if swearing an oath*) I voluntarily and of my own free will relinquish my child...forever.

CONSUELO: No! Some of us have got to get out of here right now.

MIDGE: Impossible! There's no way for us to be anywhere else, anyplace but where we are right now.

MATTIE: I never even had a boyfriend. Why do I have to have a baby when I never even had a boyfriend?

NURSE JACOBS: I voluntarily—

PARKER: You hear it? You hear it? You hear it? Finally escaping.
Can you hear the song I'm breaking into, breaking into, breakingintobreakingintobreakinginto—

WILMA: O, god! Ahhhhhh my baby's coming! Uhhhhhhhhhhhh!

PASHA: I suckled a thousand men—

WILMA: Oooooooweeeee...the pain...it hurts... unnnnnAh—

NURSE JACOBS: Call my daughter my niece forever—

CONSUELO: Mother...tell my mother he's not here—

WILMA: OhhhhhhhhhhhhAHHHHHHHHHOHHHHHH-WEEEEE uhhhhhhhhhhh!

PARKER: youhearityouhearityouhearityouhearit-youhearityouhearit?

WILMA: Ogod the PAIN it huRTS!
UhhhhhhhhhhhhoooooooooOOOOOOOOO-Uhhhhhhhhsssssssssssss
I WISH I COULD SING!

(WILMA *screams an unearthly sound, half song, half animal pain all mixed up in one long note at the exact instant a note is blown on the saxophone. Both sounds fade away as* PARKER *dies. Darkness)*

CHARLIE CHAN: *(V O)*
While unfinished women cry in no man's land
The Bird dies in a gilded cage
Could a baby's cry
Be Bird's musical notes
That hang in the air...forever?

(Curtain)

END OF PLAY